To Leah and Anora –
Meet the Boy King –
Cheryl

Tutankhamen Speaks

Cheryl Carpinello

Cheryl
Carpinello

Tutankhamen Speaks © 2013 by Cheryl Carpinello

Cover design by Berge Design

First Ebook Edition 2013
First Print Edition 2014

Copyedited by Lousie Guillaudeu
Layout & Production by ePrintedBooks & Cheryl Carpinello

Printed in the USA by Creatspace
ISBN: 978-1496155368

To Egypt,
Land of Magic and Mystery

Table of Contents

**Books in the
Tales & Legends for Reluctant
Readers Series**

Guinevere: On the Eve of Legend (lexile level: 750L)
Guinevere: At the Dawn of Legend (lexile level: 750L)
Guinevere: The Legend (Upcoming)

Young Knights of the Round Table: The King's Ransom (Book 1) (lexile level: 720L)

Sons of the Sphinx (lexile level: 620L HL)
Tutankhamen Speaks (lexile level: 840L)

Other works by Cheryl Carpinello

Short Stories:
Guardian of a Princess & Other Shorts

Early Reader:
Grandma's Tales: Wild Creatures in my Neighborhood and What If I Went to the Circus

Tutankhamen Speaks

The Letter

Dear _____,

Long ago the old texts of ancient Egypt alluded to a scroll in which King Tut spoke to the people from beyond the tomb. Many archeologists put this down to an incorrect translation of the ancient Egyptian texts. Others swore to accuracy of the translation. None of that mattered because the scroll in question could not be found. Scholars labeled it a hoax, something that never existed. It was ludicrous to imagine someone speaking from the grave. They were wrong on both accounts.

While helping to clean out a basement room in the Cairo Museum after the Arab Spring, I found an old scroll wrapped in linen and stuffed in a box. Upon further examination of said scroll, I decided to translate it myself, being, as you know, an expert in Egyptian hieroglyphs and scripts. What I found convinced me that this was the missing scroll of Tutankhamen's voice from the grave.

The condition of the text varies from well preserved to hardly able to read. In several instances, large chunks of the text were totally eroded away. Some entries had only a beginning sentence or two while others had no ending. It was the details given that convinced me that King Tutankhamen did indeed speak from beyond the tomb, from the Land of Everlasting Life. But I will leave you to decide for yourself. I don't think you'll be disappointed. If you agree with me, I urge you to publish what I have sent so that the world can see this important time-altering work.

Yours Sincerely,
S. L. Wood

Author/Editor's Note:

Several years ago I met the Egyptian scholar S.L. Wood at a lecture on the state of Egyptian antiquities in the 21st century. We talked over dinner about our fascination with and love of ancient Egypt. Over the intervening years, I received emails apprising me of items of significance he had come across. You see, Wood spent his hours in museum basements, not in the field. "Treasures," he told me, "are hidden deep in the basements of museums around the world."

One day a package arrived from him. His accompanying letter (part of which you've already read) explained what he had sent. Blown away by what I read, I've followed his wishes and published his find for the world to read and marvel about.

I've edited Wood's translation of Tutankhamen's words into chapters, giving the translation more of a story format. This was done entirely for readers' enjoyment. I also chose to use 'aten' to show the time of the Aten worship, and 'amen' or 'amun' to show Tut and Ankhesenpaaten's return to Amun's worship.

As Wood stated in his letter, pages of text were either missing or damaged. In instances where what remained ignited my interest, I have included those.

Here's hoping you will enjoy this rare peek into the life of the ancient Egyptian pharaoh King Tut!

Tutankhamen Speaks
(Stories from My Life)

Father and Me

Do you have favorite memories from your childhood that you can't bear to let go, that immediately transport you back to that time and place you will remember forever and ever? I have two that happened on the same day.

I was six years old and barefoot in the middle of winter. This I remember because the sand and stones did not burn blisters on my feet. My hands could touch the granite blocks in the square without recoiling like a snake does when its rest is disturbed in the heat.

That morning I remember waking up to a shrill noise echoing off the walls in my chamber and down the halls.

My half sister Ankhesenpaaten came running into my bedroom.

"Tutankhaten, Tutankhaten, you must get up!"

"What is that noise?" I asked, struggling to put on my tunic as she entered.

"It is an elephant! One the generals brought it this morning as a gift for Father."

"An elephant? Wherever did he find one?"

"I don't know. Come quickly, or we shall miss it!" she shouted back as she ran out of the room.

I followed her down the hallway, the roaring whistle increasing the closer we got to our father's receiving room. Rushing into the arched entrance lined with pictographs of the Aten, my father's god, our bodies froze, our eyes not believing what we beheld.

There stood the biggest animal we had ever seen.

"Tutankhaten, do you see it? Do you believe such a magnificent creature is here, in our palace?" Ankhesenpaaten was breathless after the rush down the hallway, but it didn't stop her from running on about the elephant.

And it was magnificent!

It stood there, its smooth gray skin dripping sweat. The enormous legs and feet shifted nonstop in agitation. Ears as big as me flapped nervously as its head, too small in proportion to the body, swung back and forth, its tiny eyes seeking a way out. At the front of the head was its long trunk framed by the biggest tusks I'd ever seen.

Suddenly, the trunk arched and stretched. The noise that had wakened me now blasted out of that trunk and threatened to deafen all in the room, including Ankhesenpaaten and me.

Our father stood and motioned at the door. He spoke, but no one could hear a word.

A man appeared from the other side of the animal. He was dressed in the long white gown worn by those who made the plains of sand their home. He touched the gray beast on the left side. The animal ceased its trumpeting, turned around, and followed the man out the door. That was when I saw the tail. What a funny addition to such a large animal! The tail was puny, short, and sickly looking. If the head of this animal was too small for the enormous body, then its tail was woefully out of place. It was too short to be of any use flicking away flies and gnats and couldn't even reach halfway up the body.

I looked questioningly at my father. Noticing me, he nodded his head in the direction the creature had gone. Then he did a strange thing. He held out his hand to me.

I can't remember another time that he'd ever exhibited such affection toward me. Usually he reserved that for my half-sisters. Ankhesenpaaten squeezed my arm and gave me a push in Father's direction.

A grin spread across my entire face. I might have even skipped to him. I know my heart was skipping.

Placing my tiny hand in his, strong delicate fingers wrapped around mine. A smile even touched his lips as he gently tugged on my arm.

Hand in hand we walked out of the palace and into the pleasant Egyptian winter sunlight in full view of all his subjects, who had also heard the deafening noise and had gathered to view the elephant. Ankhesenpaaten followed at Father's heels not attempting to hide the smile on her face.

This day was the day that my father the Pharaoh Akhenaten acknowledged me as his rightful heir to the throne of Egypt. Me, Tutankhaten. However, this is not the main reason I remember this day.

The Zoo

The second reason that I remember this day is that Ankhesenpaaten and I discovered that our father had his own ZOO!

The elephant shuffled down a narrow road away from the palace. My father still held tightly to my hand. He walked erect, glancing and nodding to his followers lining the roadside. Expressions on the people's faces must have mirrored my own. Disbelief at the creature lumbering ahead of us. I didn't know then that part of that disbelief was directed at me.

Ignorantly happy, I skipped along until a slight tug at my hand made me stop. I looked up into my father's eyes and saw a slight shake in answer. I was to do no more skipping. Somewhat subdued, I held my excitement inside, sure my entire body would burst with wonder and anticipation.

We walked for about twenty minutes. Quite a length of time and totally unheard of the summer. Here in the shadow of my father's regal self, I walked, warmed by the heat of the winter sun on my skin.

I had never been this far, or in this direction from the palace. Until now, I had been restricted to the large garden and play area at the back of the palace. There my half-sisters and I would run and hide for hours, even in the scorching summer sun. The tall leafy ferns, trees, and papyrus provided cool protection even at midday. I thought the garden to be the best place in the world with its shades of green and brilliant blue, red, and yellow flowers mixed around. A stream diverted from the Nile gave us excitement as we imagined exploring its banks as it wound through the trees and flowers. Sometimes we would launch wooden boats made for us by Father's builder. We would watch as the boats traveled down. Sometimes we would throw small rocks and mud balls, imagining them to be the dreaded hippo that could destroy a boat and kill all aboard in a matter of minutes as it erupted from underneath the bow.

As we continued walking, a glance around revealed that the people were falling in behind as we passed. I looked, but couldn't see the end of them.

We stopped before a set of double doors made of polished wood with two golden handles. My father turned to Ankhesenpaaten and smiled at her. Then he nodded and her delicate fingers intertwined with mine. We watched as the elephant was led around to the right, following a fence made of bound reeds and columns of granite blocks.

Father released my hand. He stepped up and with a flourish of his arms, grasped the golden handles and pushed open the heavy gates.

We stood there, our eyes growing wider. My mouth fell open in what was, I'm sure, an unprince-like manner. I tried to talk, but my voice was silent. A glance at Ankhesenpaaten confirmed her astonishment.

Before us, cages made of granite, reeds, and silken ropes filled the area and continued on beyond our sight!

A cacophony of sounds assaulted my small ears. Braying, snorting, screeching, whinnying, and bawling greeted us. Above, winged creatures I never knew existed rode the currents of a gentle breeze. Tails of every color danced across the cerulean sky, their beauty and grace stunning. Others exhibited an ugliness I hoped never to see again.

Ankhesenpaaten and I left our father's side and raced down the rows to cage after cage, careful to examine each one fully. There were lions and gazelles, ostriches and jackals, wildebeests and zebras which I recognized from the royal scribes' drawings.

Further on the sweet scent of the Nile drew us. There, in cages with the mighty river flowing through, lived those feared crocs and the menacing hippos. Up close, the terror they could bring was evident. No longer would I imagine my toy boats being destroyed. I would be able to see it happen clearly in my mind. I marveled at the vicious jaws of the crocs full of sharpened hungry teeth eager to find a man's leg, arm, or body to feast on. I imagined what it would be like to have those teeth sink into my flesh, and I shuddered at the thought.

At the end of the large enclosure in a cage with higher sides than all the rest stood the largest giraffe in the world. The tawny spots on its hide were bigger than my hand spread out wide. Opposite it in a cage re-enforced with two layers of granite blocks and thick rope, two rhinos waited, pawing the dried ground, unsure of what was happening. Ankhesenpaaten turned away as something else caught her eye.

Behind the giraffe cage, a double door

opened from the outside. In walked the man with his gray beast. I heard the gasp from the people. I heard them whisper the word--elephant. They had not known for sure. I still had trouble believing that an elephant was standing here!

The elephant raised its trunk. Quickly Ankhesenpaaten and I covered our ears. The noise of its welcome to the zoo rang throughout the enclosure. I glanced at the others and saw them scrambling to block out its trumpeting. Ankhesenpaaten and I burst out laughing in childhood amusement.

After discovering this wonderful zoo, I made it a point to visit the animals everyday. Most of the time, Ankhesenpaaten came with me. But when I found myself alone, I looked at them and wondered how they would look out in the wild. I hoped that one day I would be able to see such magnificent creatures as these outside my father's zoo.

Growing up in Akhet-Aten

From the time I was able to walk, I had the run of our palace. Usually it was just me and Ankhesenpaaten. We played the normal childhood games. We ran through the palace chasing and hiding from each other. The gardens and the pools were great places to hide. All too often one of us would fall into one of the pools as we raced by. Then we would move the game outside into the heat so that our clothes would dry. In Egypt's heat, it didn't take long. [missing text]

Sailing toy boats

When I was small, palace carpenters made me toy boats. Sometimes these were made to resemble the barges that would carry crops and animals down and up the Nile from one settlement to another. Some were fully outfitted royal barges complete with sails and the poles used when the barge was moving up river. I started playing with these in the palace pools. Later as I got better at loading them and maneuvering them, I would find a place near the palace where the Nile ran slower. There I would dig out canals for the boats to float in. Sometimes Ankhesenpaaten would help me. One time we had so many canals built that it took all afternoon for our crop barges and the royal barges to enter into the canal system and then sail through and re-enter the Nile. I loved those days with Ankhesenpaaten and the Nile.

Senet

In the evenings we would play Senet. My sisters and I became skilled Senet players, and our games would often last late into the night. [damaged text] My favorite were the casting sticks.[damaged text]

Chariots

Father had his craftsmen build us small chariots. Ankhesenpaaten and I would race around the streets of Akhet-Aten and sometimes at the edge of the great sand sea. We loved to go fast, weaving through the narrow alleyways and careening around corners. Luckily for the people, the donkeys that pulled our chariots couldn't go that fast! [damaged text]

Hunting

As I grew older, I began to hunt the birds and other animals that inhabited the banks of the Nile. When I could, I would set traps in the papyrus to catch baby crocodiles. I had to be careful because if any of the priests caught me, I would be punished. As it was, Ankhesenpaaten would lecture me anytime she thought I had been out on the papyrus. [ed. note: The crocodile was the embodiment of Sobek, the god of power, protection, and fertility.] To catch one was bad enough, but to kill one would have brought the full wrath of the priests upon me, especially after my father died, and we had moved back to Thebes. I may have been the Pharaoh, but I still liked my childhood adventures.

I went hunting for the first time in the desert for lions and jackals when I became Pharaoh around the age of ten. Ay, my grandmother's brother and Ankhesenpaaten's grandfather, accompanied me. We rode out on chariots with a driver each. These were not the chariots of my youth, nor were they the heavy chariots meant to withstand battle. My chariot was bigger than the one I raced with Ankhesenpaaten. I insisted on driving at least until our prey was sighted. Then I turned the reins over to my driver, a boy older than me with the strength to maneuver the horse, no donkey this time, to follow the tracks of the lion. I killed a lion with my spear, and returned home in triumph and with a new respect from my people.

Window of Appearances

I remember watching the ceremonies where my father and Nefertiti rewarded their loyal subjects and advisors with great interest. Above the entrance to the palace at Akhet-Aten, high in the wall, two windows stood on opposite sides of the archway. Akhenaten and Nefertiti would shower gifts of honor down upon the chosen. Sometimes these were golden collars or gowns adorned with gold and jewels. By using the window of appearances, it would seem that the gold was actually being received from the Aten. I saw the scribe Any and father's vizier Ay receive their golden gifts.

Some afternoons when the palace guards relaxed their vigil and most of the people napped to avoid the heat, Ankhesenpaaten and I would climb the stairs up to the windows.

Looking out, we could see over the tops of buildings far to the East where the Aten appeared each morning.

"Where would you go, Ankhesenpaaten, if you could leave Egypt?" I asked one afternoon.

Her eyes sparkled, and her smile widened. I watched as she rested her chin on her arms, her eyes drawn beyond the eastern horizon.

"I would travel beyond the beginnings of our land," she said.

I looked at her questioningly.

"In the women's quarters, one hears stories," she explains. "A few of the women are from there. The tales they have told are wonderful!" She turned to me then. "Imagine Tutankhaten, pools of sparkling water surrounded by lush, green bushes and trees, flowers of pink, orange, white, and even black!"

"How is that different from here?" I asked.

"Here it is only along the Nile where the bushes, reeds, and flowers grow. There in the land they call Persia exists a city where gardens hang from cliffs and mountain sides! I would love to see such a sight."

A few years later, I remembered her wish. After we were married, I had a section of our palace in Thebes reconstructed to resemble those hanging gardens that she so wished to see. Had we been given more time, I would have ventured outside of Egypt's borders and taken Ankhesenpaaten to see the gardens in person.

The Sphinx Talks

My father was not a popular leader in his time. People blamed him for everything that went wrong. Rumors spread through the town that he had cursed his people by abandoning their gods in favor of his god the Aten, a god of the sun. Forsaking the other gods upset the Maat, or the order of his people's lives.

Early on I realized that my father was not happy in Luxor, but when we moved to Akhet-Aten, he became more so. He changed his name from Amenhotep to Akhenaten in honor of that god. He even changed my name for a while to Tutankhaten. [ed. note: It is widely thought that Tutankhamen was born in Al-Amarna, what Tut calls Akhet-Aten. This could be a translation error.]

One day after the discovery of his zoo, my

father took me aside and explained some of what was happening.

"There will come a time, son, when your turn to rule Egypt is at hand," he said. "You need to understand why I embrace the god Aten, but also that I have not abandoned all the other gods."

"I am listening, my Royal Father."

And so he began a story about the mighty Sphinx of Giza so fascinating that I hoped to hear the Sphinx speak as it once did to Tuthmosis IV when I visited there.

"When I was about your age, Tutankhaten, my father took me aside and told me this story. This was before my older brother passed into the other world."

I nodded. My half-sisters had mentioned that my father was the second son.

"When I heard the story, I embraced the god Aten, determined to devote my life to his service. Then my brother met with a fatal accident out on the desert."

Here my father paused. I was never sure if it was sadness at the passing of his brother, or at the realization his life did not turn out as he had envisioned.

Amenhotep II and his Great Wife Tio lived in Memphis near the Giza Plateau. Their son Tuthmosis...[ed. note: The italics are mine to better show the story.]

"Your grandfather."

Yes. Tuthmosis would often go out hunting along the Nile and near the pyramids and the great Sphinx on the Giza plateau.

"What did they hunt, Father?"

"They sought lions and jackals. Giza teemed with these, and it was considered to be a great show of courage to kill either, as both were vicious animals."

"Father?"

"Yes?"

"Did Tuthmosis also fish in the Nile? I have seen the fish swimming there, but we never eat them."

"No, son. Now, as back then, the eating of fish is forbidden by the gods."

"Why?"

"Long ago when the gods and Egypt were young, Osiris fought with his brother Seth and lost. Seth then cut up Osiris' body and threw the parts into the Nile where the rilapia and abdju fish ate up the evidence of his betrayal. Since then, all pharaohs and priests have been forbidden to eat fish out of respect for Osiris."

"When I become pharaoh, I will not eat fish either, Father."

"That is a good son."

"What about Tuthmosis?"

"Ah yes."

One day, Prince Tuthmosis went out hunting lion and ostriches...

"Where did the ostriches come from?" My father exhibited great patience with me, his only son.

"The ostriches roamed onto Giza from the great desert to the West. When this happened, great hunting parties would be formed. The ostrich was prized highly for its beautiful feathers."

The day before rumors came to the palace that ostriches had been sighted near the pyramids. It was Tuthmosis' hope to come home with two prizes: a lion and an ostrich.

Early the next day, he and his hunting party traveled by chariot to Giza. After a morning under the burning sun and with no sign of the animals, they rested in shadow of the great Sphinx. Tuthmosis rested in the shade between the Sphinx's legs. Its mighty head blocked the intense heat.

"Will I ever get to travel to the pyramids and see the place where he slept?"

"One day, son."

All around Giza, the silence stretched as far as the sands ran. The wind was calm. Huddling down beneath the paws, Prince Tuthmosis let the stillness lull him to sleep.

"Is that when the Sphinx talked to him?"

"Yes, it was. This is what it said:

'Look upon me, my son Tuthmosis! It is I, your father, Horemakhet Kepri Re Atum. I give you your power over all Egypt. Both its White Crown and its Red Crown shall sit upon your brow...'

'You must clear this desert sand from my limbs and protect me from further damage. Long have I awaited your coming, my son. Forever will I watch over you!' [ed. note: Several variations of Tuthmosis' dream can be found in Egyptian and archeological texts.]

Then the Sphinx spoke no more.

"Ever?"

"Ever."

When Prince Tuthmosis awoke, he remembered the words spoken but told no one.

When he became Pharaoh after his father's death. Prince Tuthmosis did as the Sphinx had asked. He cleared away the sand and built a wall around it to protect it through the centuries. Then he adopted the symbol of the Aten for his standard.

"I've seen that. It's the sun with the rays coming out of it. It is on the entrance door into the palace."

"And many other places also, son."

Prince Tuthmosis put the Aten's symbol of a sun with the rays coming out of it on his standards to honor Re Horemakhet more than before. He ruled for thirty-three years.

I grew silent at that, knowing that the Aten was truly powerful to allow Tuthmosis to rule that long.

"Since that time, son, the devoted worship of the Aten has passed down from Tuthmosis to Amenhotep III, your grandfather, to me and now to you. All of us are Sons of Aten, just as

Prince Tuthmosis was."

After hearing that story, I imagined the Prince sleeping beneath the Sphinx's giant paws and hearing the god talk to him. I could understand how important it was for my family to honor the Aten. It wasn't until later that I found myself unable to continue that worship.

My Father Disturbs Maat [ed. note: Maat is the balance of the world]

Some time later I again found myself in my father's company, a common happening since the day I walked hand in hand with him to his zoo.

"Tutankhaten, I want to you understand when you are older, why I have done as I have as the Pharaoh of Egypt."

"Yes, Royal Father."

"I became enamored with the story of Prince Tuthmosis and the great Sphinx. All I wanted to do from the time I heard the story was to serve out my life in the service of my god father Re-Horemakhet."

"Didn't you want to be the pharaoh?"

"No, it was my older brother's position, not mine. However, the gods had a different and harder path for me."

"What was that, Father?"

"I was crowned pharaoh upon the death of my father and the earlier death of my brother. I was expected to continue leading the people in the open worship of Amun and maintain the Maat. I could not."

I remember looking at him, puzzled. Becoming the pharaoh of all Egypt seemed a magnificent thing.

"Before my Great Royal Wife Nefertiti and I moved here from Thebes, we were not happy. Ruling Egypt was something I was not good at, or really interested in. Even now as we speak, Grandmother Tiye handles the majority of the duties from Thebes. She has been doing so for quite a while now. Do you know why we left Thebes?"

"No, Royal Father."

"For the first time in my family's history of rulers, threats were being made against a pharaoh and his family rising from my perceived lack of leadership at the helm of Egypt."

Even at the age of six, I knew that this was very unusual and not to be talked about outside of this room. In Egypt, the pharaoh was considered to be the embodiment of a living god. For Egyptians to voice or even think about harming their pharaoh was equivalent to voicing or thinking about harming their god. Now as I think back on it, my father's worship of the Aten was just a part of their anger. Their Egypt was changing, and they didn't want that.

"Some of the people have become angry that Tiye is in charge of the armies and refuses to send the armies to protect Egypt's borders. However, Queen Tiye is doing what I asked of her. Nefertiti has helped with some additional duties, but since we've moved here, she has been busy raising our children."

I nodded as if I understood all that he told me, but some of it was beyond my six years.

"I love Egypt and her people, Royal Son, but I have never wanted to rule her. I hope that the people of Egypt and you will understand that in time."

I did eventually, but it was several years after this conversation, and after many other events had occurred.

My father was not popular with the Egyptian people because he chose to devote his life to worship of the Aten. He did not turn his back on the rest of our gods, he just continued the worship inspired by Tuthmosis and the Sphinx. Many felt that this worship combined with his refusal to arm Egypt's borders disrupted Maat that pharaohs were responsible to maintain.

I sometimes felt that Father was as disappointed in the Egyptian people as they were in him. He expected them to respect and honor his commitment to Tuthmosis. It is true that the temples in Thebes, particularly at Karnak, appeared to close down, but not through any orders of my father. When the people followed him to Akhet-Aten, that left few worshippers in Thebes.

It was just a year after discovering my father's zoo that life changed for both of us. His final act as Pharaoh, driven by his lack of ambition to rule Egypt, has baffled people who came after. He, however, saw it as a way to honor his duties as Pharaoh and a follower of Aten. It involved my stepmother Nefertiti.

My Mother and Grandmother

Father told me my mother died giving me birth. She was a princess, the Princess Tadukhipa, but he called her Kiya. She came from Mitanni by Babylonia. She was one of many women in my father's harem, a group of women given to pharaohs from other countries and clans to insure peace.

It was not uncommon for pharaohs to take more than one wife. While Nefertiti was my father's Great Royal Wife, she bore him six daughters, but no sons. My father then chose Kiya to bear him a son, and she did.

My nursemaid was Maya, but it was my Grandmother Tiye that I remember the most. She doted on me when she visited and showered me with motherly love. She appointed herself and her brother Ay as my protectors, but

Grandmother was away a lot. After my father became pharaoh, she continued to oversee the military as she had done for my grandfather Amenhotep III. When I was small, she cut off a lock of her reddish-gold hair and concealed it inside of four small nesting sarcophagus coffins.

"Tutankhaten," she said. "In the innermost sarcophagus I have placed a lock of my hair which rests underneath a solid gold statue of you. Keep the coffins safe and hidden in your room. They will protect you when I am unable to."

I thanked her and prized such a gift, not only for protection, but because my grandmother's gift was wonderfully made. The outer sarcophagus was made of wood; the second of plaster covered with gold leaf; the third of wood which contained the solid gold statue of myself; the fourth again of plaster covered with gold leaf and containing my grandmother's gift.

While Grandmother Tiye held a special place in my heart, she also delivered devastating news, previously withheld by my father, shortly before his death.

"Tutankhaten," she stated one day as we sat in the garden of the palace. "You will be Pharaoh after your father dies. You should not be kept in the dark about your heritage."

I looked at her questioningly.

"I know what you've been told. Yes, you

are your father's son, but Kiya was not your mother."

I don't know what I had expected, but I was not prepared for that news.

"Though Kiya was a royal princess, even your father would not have entrusted the birth of his only son to a foreign-born princess."

"Why not? Who was my mother?"

"To bear the son of a Pharaoh of Egypt, a woman must be loyal to no other country but Egypt. Kiya loved Egypt and your father, but her home and loyalty lay with Mitanni. To be a son of Princess Tadukhipa meant that you would also be subject to the King of Mitanni and his rules. That can never happen. To rule Egypt is to be loyal to no country, no rule except Egypt."

"Why did Father lie to me?"

"When you were smaller, it seemed the best. The inner workings of a royal family can be misunderstood and not easily comprehended by one so young. For centuries in Egypt, and in other countries I would imagine, royal families have always kept the royal bloodline within the family."

"What does that mean?"

"Your father could marry whomever he wished, but to have a foreigner bear his son was not a choice presented to him. Instead he chose Queen Sitamun, my daughter and acting Great Royal Wife. His sister."

"Why don't I remember her?"

"Shortly after you were born, a sickness came into Egypt and took many of our people. My daughter and your mother Sitamun was one of these."

When my father died, I was nearly seven, and at that time, my world changed.

My Stepmother Nefertiti aka Smenkhkare

Nefertiti was named Father's Great Royal Wife when she married him. He could have chosen anyone for this because it was an adviser's position and really had nothing to do with being the actual wife of a pharaoh.

Nefertiti was a woman as strong as she was beautiful. After all, she was from her own line of royalty. She believed in and loved my father, I do know that. However, she also knew, as my father did, that Egypt needed a strong ruler.

To provide that rule, my father appointed Nefertiti as co-regent of Egypt. He had her change her given name to strengthen her rule. Nefertiti adopted the male name of Smenkhkare and dressed in the robes of a man.

For many of my early years, Nefertiti was away at Thebes. Since my father made her co-regent of Egypt, her job kept her there dealing with affairs of state. I saw her briefly when she would return to Akhet-Aten to visit father and her girls. Then, and nowhere else, she would drop the disguise of Smenkhkare, the male persona she assumed to rule Egypt. Later, historians assumed that my father had banished his beloved wife for a man, but Egypt knew who ruled her.

She was not overly friendly with me, even when in the company of my father. She enjoyed the power that came with ruling Egypt and had hoped that her daughter, Meritaten, her Great Royal Wife, would continue to rule after she was gone. That was not to be. Egyptian rule passes from father to son.   As soon as my father acknowledged my birthright, Nefertiti's time as Egypt's ruler was numbered in years, not decades.

I was considered too young to rule at seven, but there had been others before me who were younger when they became pharaoh. However, it was decided by my father's and my close adviser Ay, Nefertiti's father, that Nefertiti would rule for me until I was ten. At that time, with selected advisors, I would officially be crowned King of Egypt.

It was too bad that Nefertiti and I could not be close. I had played with her younger girls as I grew up, and one in particular held a special place in my heart. Such is the case though with a king. While Nefertiti's devotion to Egypt and its gods prevented her from doing me harm, we could not be called friends.

Tutankhamen Speaks

Who in the Heck is in Charge of Egypt?

At ten years of age, not even someone like myself, groomed my entire life to rule, would be able to do so. Upon my crowning, Ay appointed himself co-regent over Upper Egypt. At the same time, he appointed General Horemheb as co-regent over Lower Egypt. Horemheb was not happy with my father's family and how they chose to ignore the threats against Egypt. Ay was aware of this and thought the best course of action would be to keep Horemheb away from Thebes and me. And so it was done. I became a figurehead, a talisman for the people, the embodiment of all Egyptian gods. [missing further text.]

Tutankhamen Speaks

My Great Royal Wife Ankhesenpaaten

Two years after I was crowned Pharaoh, I was ready to assume my duties as the Pharaoh of Egypt. Ay also informed me that it was time that I married and named my Great Royal Wife. While this may seem unbearable to non-Egyptians, it was a perfectly acceptable custom in my time. So was the custom of those of royal blood marrying within their families to keep the bloodline in the family.

At the age of twelve, there were only two women that I loved. One was my grandmother Tiye; the other my half sister Ankhesenpaaten.

Ankhesenpaaten was fourteen at this time. We had been together for nearly twelve years, all of my life. The most natural act in the world seemed to be to ask her to marry me. I felt confident of her answer, but one never knows.

The time came as we sat together by the Nile. I had arranged for a meal that I carried as we walked to one of our favorite places where the Nile touches our father's beautiful garden at the far west end.

Although it was summer, we found shade beneath a tree and sat among the grasses on the banks. As often when we were together lately, little conversation took place. We were comfortable with each other's company and the beauty around us.

That day, I broke the silence with a hint of excitement in my voice, unfortunately, still that of a child.

"Ankhesenpaaten," I said. *"I spoke with Ay last night when he arrived back from Thebes."* [ed. note: The italics are mine.]

"How was Uncle? I did not see him this morning." [ed. note: Uncle may be a translation error as Ay was her grandfather.]

"He is fine, but he left early to travel back to Thebes to speak with the priests of Karnak."

She cocked her head and looked at me in that way of hers when she knew that something else was actually being said.

"How sad that he could not spare a moment to say hello to his favorite girl," she said somewhat reproachingly.

"He said to give you his blessing and this."

I leaned toward her and brushed my lips on her cheek. She smelled of lotus and summer and love. A unique combination I have never forgotten.

She blushed and lightly touched her cheek with her loving fingers. She dropped her head and looked at me through her silky black hair.

"Is that all Uncle said?"

I reluctantly looked away and let my gaze sweep over the mighty river in front of us, lazily following the path to the wide water to the North.

At twelve, while not the youngest ever to rule Egypt, I was certainly one of the most inexperienced.

Ay had worked hard with me since my stepmother Nefertiti had been forced out upon my father's death so that I could assume my rightful position. There was still a lot for me to learn. I understood when Ay had told me that I needed to be strong for our people and to present them with a leadership that would restore Maat and allow them to return to their way of life and worship before my father.

Ankhesenpaaten would stand by my side and support the decisions whether I made them alone or Ay convinced me of the right decisions to make. I also knew her feelings for me were as strong as mine for her. We had played together for years, and we enjoyed each other's company.

This time, however, I found myself suddenly shy and full of doubts, my heart pounding. Not much different from when you wish for something, but are afraid to see if you have gotten it, for fear of disappointment.

I turned to Ankhesenpaaten and smiled at her. Her returning smile quieted my fears, but not my heart. Before me was the one I loved and my heart raced to think of our lives together on one path.

"Ankhesenpaaten," I said. "Ay also told me that it was time, not that I needed him to tell me. All of my life, I have known in my soul that this moment would come."

I took her hands in mine and breathed in deeply the scent that was hers alone. I looked into her dark and sparkling eyes and felt the electricity racing through her fingertips. She tilted her head to look at me, and I knew what her answer would be before I asked her.

"Ankhesenpaaten, would you honor me by marrying me?"

She sighed softly, and her smile melted my heart.

"Ah Tutankhaten, you honor me with your asking."

I started to protest, but her fingers silenced my words.

"I have loved you from the beginning. As the years have progressed, I have felt that love grow stronger each day. My most precious wish has been to spend my life by your side, as your wife. Yes, I will marry you," she finished softly, the last said as her lips touched my cheek.

We turned and our lips sealed our words, our promise, and our lives.

Some may think that we were too young, but we had loved each other as children, and our love continued to grow during what would become our short life together.

Tutankhamen Speaks

Heartbreak

Can you recall a time of great sadness in your life? A time when the burden on your heart threatens to break it in two? I had two such times in my short life. My heart still aches and cries inside of me when I remember those times.

The first time occurred when I was fifteen years and in year eight of my reign. Ankhesenamun and I had been married for three years, and we were going to have a child, an heir to the throne of Egypt!

As excited as we were, we were also scared. After all, we were hardly more than children ourselves. However, our family and vizors assured us of their total support. It is not hard to raise a child, we were told, when the whole palace helped with the raising.

Alas, we did not have the opportunity to

find out. At five months of being heavy with child, Ankhesenamun took ill. She awakened in the middle of the night and rushed out in the garden where she emptied her stomach. She then collapsed on the ground. I rushed to her side.

"Ankhesenamun," I cried. "What is the matter?"

Her answer was lost in her cries.

I remember calling for Ay. He and others converged on the garden. Taking one look at Ankhesenamun, Ay called for a litter and a doctor.

I gripped Ankhesenamun's hand as she was moved, her cries still full of pain and fear.

Once inside the palace, she was taken to our room. There the doctor awaited, an anxious look on his face made only graver as he saw Ankhesenamun.

Ay consulted with him briefly, then drew me from her side.

"Tutankhamen," he said. "It is as I feared. The doctor says that she will lose the baby tonight."

Ankhesenamun let out a curdling scream. As I turned around, she tried to sit up and clutched at her stomach. Then she fell back, silent.

I tried to go to her, but Ay grabbed my arm and pulled me out of the room. Out of the corner of my eye, I saw women move from the corner of the room toward Ankhesenamun and the doctor. Then I saw no more.

Hours later, I don't know how long, the doctor came out of our room. I watched his face, trying to read what had happened in the deadly silence that followed Ankhesenamun's scream.

"Sire," the doctor said.

I stood on unsteady legs with Ay's help.

"Sire, I am deeply sorry. The queen has lost the baby girl."

I nearly collapsed, but steadied myself upon my walking stick.

"And Ankhesenamun?" I asked.

"She is tired, afraid, and sad, but otherwise she will fully recover given time."

I nodded, and he bowed and left.

Ay still stood beside me, his arm around my shoulders. I looked at him and felt the tears fill my eyes. He turned and held me close while my sobs and sorrow shook my body.

Ay didn't understand. I wasn't crying just over the loss of our child; I had been afraid that I had lost Ankhesenamun also. Later, Ankhesenamun and I would share our sorrow at the loss of our little girl.

The second time when I thought my heart would be torn apart was a little over two years later. Ankhesenamun and I were expecting another child. This time with only one month before the baby was due, Ankhesenamun clutched my hand as we sat at dinner with our honored vizor, several scribes, and priests.

Feeling her nails bite at my skin, I looked at her and saw a paleness wash over her face. My eyes questioned her, and I'll never forget her answer.

Over her face a glow followed the paleness. Her tiny mouth grimaced as she whispered to me.

"It's time Tutankhamen, it's time."

Excitement raced through my body. As I stood, I looked at our guests and proudly delivered the news.

"Friends, please excuse us, but we must leave." I looked at each one, a smile on my face. "Ay, if you will arrange for the doctor, it is time according to my Queen!"

Cheers followed us out of the room.

After the death of the first child, Ankhesenamun and I were afraid upon finding out we were again going to have a child. We spent many anxious hours in the beginning. After the fifth and then the sixth month passed, we both relaxed and enjoyed the coming event as only prospective parents can. We marveled at the movements of the child inside Ankhesenamun, so like those of a fish if one were able to rest one's hand on its fin as the fish went about its day.

We tried to hurry to our bedroom, but the

most we managed was a shuffle down the tiled halls, stopping frequently as the pains nearly doubled Ankhesenamun. The doctor waited at our door. I helped Ankhesenamun into the room and onto the couch covered with linen in preparation for the birth. I remember the doctor's hand on my shoulder, his head nodding toward the door.

I bent down and kissed Ankhesenamun's forehead and squeezed her hand. A smile crossed her red lips, and then a grimace took its place as another pain coursed through her body. Turning quickly, I left, my heart in pain at having to leave her.

Ay sat beside me on the marble bench. His second wife ***** was helping the doctor. [missing text] Only one thought filled my head. The same thought over and over. Even though Ankhesenamun and I were confident about this birth, the thought would not leave.

Each little sound carried to my ears. I heard the doctor's commands to ******. [missing text] I heard Ankhesenamun's voice distorted in pain. I heard Ay's heavy breathing at my side. I heard it all. Almost.

I looked at Ay. His head hung on his chest. His eyes could not meet mine. My breath refused to come. Shakes took over my body. I tried to stand, but my legs refused to obey me, the Pharaoh of Egypt! The ruler of the greatest country in the world could not even stand as the realization numbed my body.

The door opened. By sheer force of will, I stood and with legs stiff like the building timbers walked to the door. I heard Ankhesenamun's ragged sobs. *****'s soft words, meant to comfort. [missing text] I felt Ay's arm around my waist refusing to let me, the Pharaoh of Egypt, fall.

"I am so sorry, my Pharaoh. It was not in my power to save the child and my calls to ****received no answer." [missing text] His head was bowed nearly to his knees. His words almost mumbled. His sorrow so evident.

"What," I coughed, the words threatening to choke me. "What was the baby?"

"It would have been a daughter, Sire." He didn't lift his head, but I heard the words.

With daggers my heart was pierced. Ay's grip on me tightened. I looked through the door to Ankhesenamun lying on the couch. The once white linen now soiled with sadness and death. Her face so pale, her once beautiful emerald eyes puffy and red.

I shook off Ay's arm. Hobbling over, I knelt down beside the couch and grasped Ankhesenamun's hand. She squeezed my hand, and I squeezed back. I pressed my lips to the back of her hand. Then I lay down beside her and felt the sobs racking her wounded body. I cradled her in my arms, and my tears joined hers.

Of All the Dumb Things to Happen

My death was not spectacular. It did not involve treachery. It wasn't covered up. The record of my death was simply destroyed when General Horemheb became Pharaoh. Upon his crowning, he immediately set to destroying everything that contained Ay's name, my name, and my father's name. He obliterated everything: remade monuments to appear as his own, chiseled out every reference to us and replaced our names with his. Such was the Egyptian way.

Alas, my death which came about as men's deaths will, out of love.

I was out hunting ostriches in my chariot. Coming upon two, I gave chase. My trusted friend and one that I called uncle, Nakhtmin, drove for me as he often did when he came to

Thebes. We had such adventures and loved to chase the ostriches.

We drove south of Thebes the afternoon before, eager to be in place at first light. Three other chariots traveled with us. One brought the two dogs, lean, gray, and fast. The other two carried additional runners. Ostriches were fast but could be tired if the chase was orchestrated right.

We forded the Nile three miles south with enough of Re's light to spot the hippopotamus and crocodiles before they surprised us. Once across, we cleared the fields and made our way into the Western Desert. Nightfall found us beside a dune pile. We made a small camp and a fire with sticks carried in the chariot. Even in summer, temperatures plummeted once Re took his rest. We ate stewed figs, honey cakes, cheese, and wine. Tomorrow we planned on eating ostrich.

Just after Dawn, we started west through the desert. After an hour, the runners spotted tracks. Two ostriches were in front of us. Spreading out on either side, they quickly moved ahead to get in front of the desert birds. Then they would begin to push the ostriches toward us. The dogs would be sent once the ostriches were in our sight.

It took another two hours by the position of Re for the runners to get in front of the long-necked birds. They released a trained gray pigeon that flew directly to us. Nakhtmin signaled to the dogs, which had been racing back and forth since the pigeon returned. The dogs were not novices; they knew what the pigeon meant. Immediately they shot off and soon disappeared in the distance.

I readied the spears while Nakhtmin drove the chariot after the dogs. The horse, ready for the hunt after a morning of no excitement, enjoyed the run which was evident as he tossed his maned head throughout the chase like a small child jumping from foot to foot while waiting for a present from his grandmother. I know because I acted the same way each time Grandmother Tiye returned to Akhet-Aten to see me.

Up ahead dust appeared on the horizon. We had caught up to the dogs and hopefully, to the ostriches!

Nakhtmin whipped the horse, which needed little urging. It doubled its speed in a beat of my heart. As we neared the dust whirl, figures materialized inside. I was expecting the ostriches, but the dogs came first, running at top speed off to the side, looking to turn the birds for the final chase. Then came the birds barreling upon us like the balls the children in the village rolled down the streets with sticks.

The ostriches turned sharply to the right trying to shake the dogs. Nakhtmin followed quickly with the reins on the horse. I grabbed the side of the chariot to avoid being thrown out. Then I righted myself and readied the spear in my right hand, testing the balance.

I would only get one chance. Once the spear left my hand, Nakhtmin would have to turn the chariot in the opposite direction to avoid a collision with the downed ostrich. We would be out of position for a second throw.

Nakhtmin looked at me. I nodded. He whipped the horse a final time. The dogs spread out to either side of the ostriches, anticipating the kill. I prayed to Re to guide my spear. Taking a deep breath I launched the spear and watched as it spiraled toward the closest bird.

Something was wrong, my brain roared. Instinctively my hand reached for the railing of the chariot as Nakhtmin jerked the reins of the horse to the right behind the ostrich! A blur raced beside me, and I recognized one of the dogs. It had not gotten out of the way.

Before I could get my balance, the chariot hit the back of the ostrich as it went down on its knees. Nakhtmin shouted something at me. Through the blur in front of me, I saw his hand reaching out for me. Then we hit the ostrich! The horse attempted to jump over the ostrich's body, then went down in a heap. We collided with the bodies. The chariot's wood screamed as it cracked. Nakhtmin flew over the front and disappeared.

I struggled to stay upright, but failed. The

chariot toppled over, and then I was sailing through the air. The ground did not embrace my body. Instead it slammed against me, bones cracking, and flesh ripping.

I woke with the sun beating down on me, my head pounding, and my body screaming. As I tried to sit up, firm hands forced me back to the desert floor.

"My lord," Nakhtmin said. "You must lie still."

"How badly am I hurt?"

"You have some bruises and cuts. No, don't try to get up."

"Something more is wrong with me, isn't it? My thigh feels like Re is burning inside my flesh."

"The thigh bone is broken, my lord. I was trying to stabilize it when you came to. It's going to hurt, but I have to strap the spear shaft to your leg in order to move you."

I nodded, gritting my teeth to keep from crying out like a baby. As he tightened the shaft, I couldn't help but flinch. Then dizziness came upon me, and I passed out.

When I came to again, the sky was darkening. Re was sinking in the West.

I tried to sit up.

"My lord, let me help you."

Nakhtmin's arm slid under my back. With his assistance I sat up, wincing in pain as my leg exploded. Dizziness threatened to overcome me again, but I fought it off.

I sat up for a few moments but the pain was too intense to bear even after chewing on the bitter root Nakhtmin gave me.

"Help me to lay back down, Nakhtmin."

As I lay there, I drifted off to sleep for a while. When I woke it was dark. I could feel the coolness of the desert floor sink into my bare skin. I shivered and immediately the pain in my thigh increased with the movement.

"My lord," Nakhtmin said, "I've heated up some wine and honey cakes. The warmth will drive off the chill of the night air. Then we can see if we can move you closer to the fire and onto the plume of the ostrich to keep you off the desert floor."

I nodded, not trusting my voice to speak without betraying my pain. I chewed the honey cakes slowly, feeling each bite as it warmed every part of my body it passed through. Then I drank the wine and relished the warmth and the numbing of the pain it provided. Nakhtmin watched me closely, and when I had finished, he looked at me questioningly.

"Where are the runners?"

"Nearly back at Thebes. With luck, help will arrive tomorrow before Re reaches his zenith."

I looked over at the broken chariot. No way to get back to Thebes with that. He had made the only choice to deliver us safely to the palace.

"Thank you, Nakhtmin. Now, should we try that move?"

The next minutes were some of the most painful of my life. Actually it ended up being more like an hour. I literally inched along the desert floor toward the ostrich plume. Nakhtmin gave me a piece of my spear to bite into when it came time to lift my body onto the plume. With his help, I positioned my arms on either side of the plume. Then bracing my arms with Nakhtmin at my feet, we moved my body onto the plume. Then I abruptly passed out, not even noticing the additional warmth of the fire. [ed. note: This is the end of the translated text, possibly because after this, Tut died.]

Tutankhamen Speaks

Author/Editor's Final Note:

I leave you to judge whether what you have just read is true and happened as the ancient scrolls related.

For myself, I tend to believe that this could have happened. History is full of accounts of people speaking with the dead. Séances are not new. It is probable that King Tut did speak to someone, who is never named in the translation, and that person wrote down what he remembered the king saying.

Whether it is true or not true, it gives us something to ponder.

To My Readers

If you liked *Tutankhamen Speaks*, please be kind enough to leave a short review on the site where you purchased the book. I hope you share your reading enjoyment with friends and family.

Want to read more about Ancient Egypt? Try my historical paranormal story *Sons of the Sphinx*. I've included an excerpt at the end of this book.

About the Author

Cheryl Carpinello is a retired high school English teacher. A devourer of books growing up, her profession introduced her to writings and authors from times long past. Through her studies and teaching, she fell in love with the Ancient and Medieval Worlds. Now, she hopes to inspire young readers and those Young-at-Heart to read more through her Tales and Legends for Reluctant Readers set in these worlds. Come by and say hi!

www.cherylcarpinello.com;
Educator/Parent site:
www.beyondtodayeducator.com

Sons of the Sphinx

The Prophecy

Behold, when the last boy pharaoh is awakened, he will have one chance to right the wrong. United with a spirit vessel from the future, he must seek to find the one robbed of his reign who will lead the way to the tomb of the boy pharaoh's lost queen. There must the confrontation with the usurper be held and the presentation of his confession to the old priests be given. If the usurper holds his tenth Jubilee and is allowed to acknowledge his son as his successor, the wrong will not be righted, and the queen will remain lost to her pharaoh forever.

Tutankhamen Speaks

Chapter 1

I don't see dead people. I hear them. I talk to them. Boy, you should try that. Talk about people looking at you like you've got two heads. That will do it. I used to look in the mirror after talking to them to see what others saw. All I saw was me, Rosa, an ordinary teenage girl. No ghosts on my shoulders, no glowing auras.

It would be one thing if I talked to famous dead people. You know, like that Elvis Presley guy my mother still drools over? I mean, really? The guy would be, like, ancient today! Anyway, if I talked to him, I could give my mom a personal message like, "Sorry we never got to hook up." That would be worth a few extra bucks for allowance, don't you think?

No, the dead people who talk to me are just dead nobodies. Nothing exciting to say. Nothing going down. They're just hanging out; waiting for—I don't know—to be more dead, I guess. Or to see how much trouble they can get me in.

Take today in math class. We're taking this test, see. I'm concentrating real hard on this problem trying to figure height or something. Then I hear this:

"Hey you."

I jerk up in my chair, searching for the guy doing the talking. I glance at the kids on either side of me. Nothing. I look up at the teacher. He's glaring at me.

"Great," I whisper. "He probably thinks I'm trying to cheat." I bow my head and focus on the problem again.

"You, I'm talking to you."

I shake my head in hopes of tossing the voice out. I know now. Some dumb dead guy wants to talk to me.

"Would you be quiet? I'm trying to take a math test."

"Oh sure, that's okay for you to say. I'll never take another test again." His voice breaks up like bad radio reception.

"Not my problem."

"I died too soon, I really did."

"Look, I haven't talked to one yet who didn't say that. Kind of goes with the dead part. Now leave me alone. You're going to make me fail this test."

I hear him snort like he has to blow his nose, if the dead can actually do that. Then comes the kicker.

"I just want another chance. I promise I'll do better."

"I'm going to say this one more time. Not my problem. Now leave me alone." I form three exclamation points in my head so if he is reading my thoughts as well as listening, he will get the

picture.

"But it isn't fair," he whines. *"It just isn't fair."*

Okay. I'm fed up with this guy. I can't even remember the formula for whatever answer I'm trying to find. I am definitely going to fail if he keeps on yapping. I try to ignore him and concentrate on remembering that formula.

"Not fair."

My brain is fried, and I've had enough. I slam my pencil on my desk and stand up. "Bud, I don't give a damn if it isn't fair. Just shut the hell up so I can get this test done!"

Did you get the part where I "stand up and yell"? Yep, that earns me an F on the test AND a trip to the AP's office. I can't even defend myself. What am I going to say? "Excuse me, I'm sorry I blurted out loud in the middle of a test, and I'm sorry for cussing, but you see, this dead person wouldn't shut up." Yeah, that would go over well. Nope, I just sit with my head down, my face burning from embarrassment, and whisper, "It won't happen again. Had to be the stress over the test." You get the picture.

The rest of the day I endure the strange looks and whispers by shrugging and mumbling something like "Idiot dead people." The kids will avoid me for the next few days. I think they're afraid whatever I have will rub off on them, or that I've gone bananas or something. Understandable.

All this comes from my grandmother Nana. When I was little, she lived with us, and it was like Halloween every night. She told the most amazing stories about spirits that visited her. Nana said I would inherit her gift, except it's not a gift. It is definitely a curse. Because of it, I had the first and last sleepover at my house in the third grade when Nana decided to share one of her stories with my best friend Rachel and me. In the years since Nana passed away, I've been laughed at, shunned, and avoided, especially after an incident like today.

When my parents get home and hear what happened...Well I might be the one shouting "It's not fair."

So now I sit in my bedroom trying to work on a history project. You know, the kind where the teacher puts you in a group, and then no one in the group does anything? Yep, that's my luck. This is due the day after tomorrow, and no one except me has done anything. I'll probably fail if it's not finished. My eyes wander around the room instead of focusing.

"Roosa."

Without thinking, I blurt out, "It's Rosa, not Roosa. And I told you to get lost. Now." I jump to the door and slam it shut. Do the dead have no respect?

And just who is THIS guy? It's not the same person who got me in trouble at school. That's nice. Now I have an army of dead people invading my brain. Too bad they can't do this project for me.

"Roosa."

Who is this idiot?

"Listen. This is my room, my space. These are my things, and I refuse to share them with dead people!"

I jump on top of my bed; I'm just getting warmed up. It has been a stressful day.

"These are my favorite books on this bookcase. See, my marked up copy of *The Once and Future King*. Here is my *The Black Stallion* series. And, here, my Grandpa's National Geographics where I first read about King Tut. All mine!"

I think I'm going nuts. Who rants and raves at the dead? Shaking with frustration, I jump down and sit at my desk. The stupid history project stares back at me. At least it's on ancient Egypt. Something I'm interested in.

"Roosa."

Will this guy never give up?

We're supposed to chronicle the reigns of the 18th Dynasty and evaluate the successes/failures of each pharaoh. I chose King Tutankhamen. Mom took me to the Tut exhibit when it toured the US. Talk about magnificent! I still have my ticket stub pinned on the wall above my desk.

"Roosa."

"I hear nothing."

King Tut ruled Egypt at the age of nine over thirty-five hundred years ago. It wasn't until 1922 that his hidden burial site was discovered by Howard Carter.

Next to the Tut ticket is my favorite picture of Ankhesenamun and Tut. You know the one: it's on the back of the Golden Throne. He's sitting in the throne; she's standing facing him, one arm outstretched, touching him. I'm not a romantic — well, maybe a little. The point is, in that picture, the love they feel for each other is so obvious. I'm going to use it for the presentation. It's the one item that shows them as real people, not just a part of history.

I like looking at that picture. Sometimes I even imagine myself as Ankhesenamun. I know, I have no life. You try being in tenth grade and living with a curse. See how many boyfriends you have.

Sometimes I think they are discussing their future. You know, how many children they'll have, and how they'll raise them. Maybe they talk about what's happening in Egypt, and she shows her support with a simple touch on his hand. They could also be talking about where they'll be buried. They did that, you know. Had their burial chambers ready years before their death.

On days like today when I'm feeling depressed — the curse will do that to me — it could be Ankhesenamun is saying goodbye to

Tut as he dies. She assures him they will meet in the Afterlife. What would it be like to wander the earth looking for my husband's spirit or *ba?* Does Tut look for her's?

"I do, Roosa."

I turn around and scream.

Sons of the Sphinx: sold wherever books are found.